PAIN IS DEAF

PAIN IS DEAF

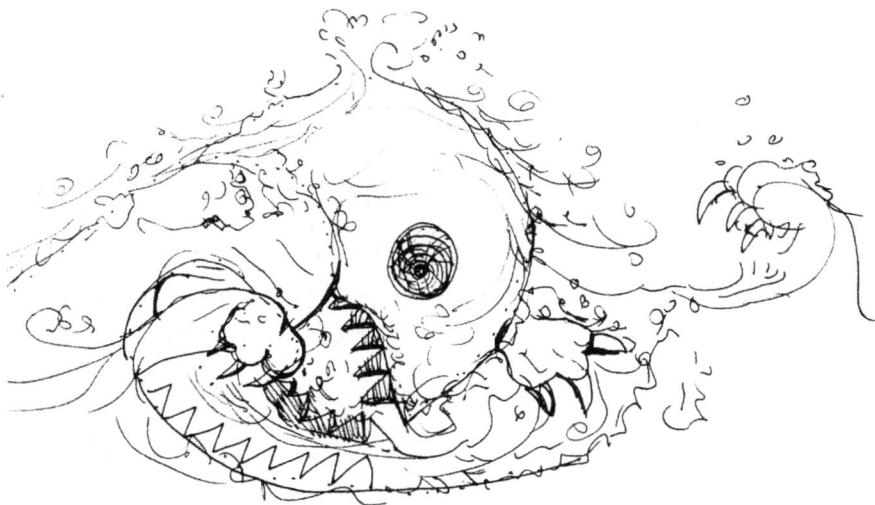

Revised and expanded edition.

LAURA MOLET ESTAPER
Translated by Montserrat Barragán

IPBOOKS.net
International Psychoanalytic Books

International Psychoanalytic Books (IPBooks)
New York • http://www.IPBooks.net

Published by IPBooks, Queens, NY

Online at: www.IPBooks.net

ISBN 978-1-969031-01-4

Image created by *Victoria Madrigal* ©

No surrender to the fear and suffering when the devil dresses up as the abuser and cancer.

Laura Molet Estaper

*Equality, justice and
freedom without anger.*

*Security, strength and
freedom without bitterness or anger.*

*Courage, bravery and
freedom without resentment or anger.*

*Hope, compassion and
freedom without fear or anger.*

*Resilience, coherence and
freedom without pain or anger.*

Freedom free from the chains of anger.

Contents

FOREWORD AND ACKNOWLEDGEMENTS

I am rewriting these acknowledgements, formulating and reflecting on my thoughts, while imagining all of you future readers. When you read these pages, it will be your present, and this moment will have passed. And yet, now you are here with me, and I am speaking to you as I write, anticipating the future as it happens with the prospective function (Atlas Aron 2018).

We are now presenting a revised, expanded, translated edition of my book *Pain is Deaf* (2018). I want to thank Ruth Lijtmaer, "my good enough mother," for her perseverance, insistence, and patience in ensuring this translation. When we presented the book at an international IARPP conference in Tel Aviv in 2019, we realized the book deserved to be translated so that the English-speaking population could read it. I feel fully satisfied and proud of both the revised/expanded Spanish volume as well of this English version of the book.

Without Montserrat's Barragán enthusiasm, interest, and willingness to review and translate the book, I believe it would have been much harder for me to embark on this new adventure. Then came the COVID-19 pandemic, with the isolation it brought, the widespread fear we felt, the context of insecurity and uncertainty we lived through, and the disconnection we experienced on so many levels—physically, relationally, and most of all, emotionally. Many of our projects were abandoned or postponed. Finally, I have been able to resume one of them, so that it would not remain just an idea or an illusion to be materialized.

And so finally, here and now, you have these revised and translated pages, created with dedication and pleasant surprises, as several of the most significant women who have accompanied me over the last six years have joined the project. Thank you all for your words and contributions that enrich the original book, resulting in a choral book of women's voices that dare to give voice to pain: Galit Atlas, Montserrat Barragán, Victoria Font Saravia, Yanina Piccolo, Alejandra Plaza.

I also feel immense gratitude toward María Teresa González de Garay Fernández for her extraordinary attention to the details in every paragraph of the book, and to Mar Valldeoriola for helping me think through and seek internal coherence across the different sections and chapters, giving meaning to pain.

A very special and heartfelt acknowledgement goes to Mayte González López for believing in this book, supporting it unconditionally, and for trusting and believing in me in the way only she knows how.

This is a very special edition. Using Yanina Piccolo's accurate definition, this is an "intervened book"—a book in which more professionals intervene and add their voices, helping to provide an outlet for the deaf and deafening pain.

This volume is dedicated to the people who have suffered and to those who still suffer. It aims to be an accompaniment and help to "dare to be oneself", to have the initiative and make the right decisions at every moment, from the freedom of choice and coherence with active internal agency, turning us into survivors or heroines, leaving behind the passive agency that keeps us stuck in the role of victims.

And there is a way out.
There is a way out of pain.
There is a way out of barbarism.

I owe this learning on the one hand to my patients, from whom day after day and session after session I learn. They learn, and we learn so much together. To *each and every* one of them, I send a message of gratitude for having co-created such intense spaces for so many shared experiences and emotions lived and felt.

Especially to my patient Helen, whose pain and suffering we have been identifying and transforming on her long way to freedom (I thank her for giving me permission to publish and share her story, her life experience). Thank you, Victoria Madrigal, for this extremely graphic cover, which captures the essence of the Tumorized Emotional Tsunami T. E. T. (Bromberg 2011; Molet 2018).

And on the other hand, to Life: to the experiences it stores for us, some better than others, to the setbacks that come when you least expect them, and above all, how we manage to get out of these situations —what resources we use, what tools we have (or do not have), whether we are therapists and/or patients. Difficulties, trauma, illnesses, losses—these are all intertwined and interconnected throughout the book between the genuine and authentic experiences of patients, especially Helen's, and my own.

This book also aims to be a hymn to freedom. And to love: giving it and receiving it. As Joan Coderch (2017) says: "Love is not enough, but without love, nothing will be sufficient."

It is an anthem of equality of conditions between man and woman, woman and man, man and man, woman and woman; Subject to Subject, where one does not submit the other, and the other is not the one submitted. There is mutual and reciprocal influence, as in every relational exchange, where one remains oneself and the other as well, without trying to change, condition, threaten, or dominate the other. A relationship based on equity, respect, and equality (Benjamin 1988).

Six intense years have passed since I wrote the first edition of *Pain is Deaf,* and during this time many things have happened, inherent to the simple fact of living. Some have been bad—very significant losses—others neither good nor bad, and some others very good, such as the "cure" of cancer (for now) and the creation of Relational Home. It has been a period of great professional expansion, both national and internationally, which has given me the opportunity to meet great people, excellent professionals, and to create new and significant bonds.

Relational Home is a space for therapy, teaching, and learning—a dream come true. The name of the center is inspired by the concept defined by R. Stolorow (2005), which refers to the human context of embracement and emotional understanding that allows the validation, acceptance, and holding of traumatized states of consciousness. It is a warm, intimate place that invites the construction of bonds of trust that result in healing therapeutic actions that allow the development of the authenticity of each patient who consults. Where emotional orphanhood reigned, emotional connection will take place, and a true Relational Home—one that identifies, accepts, supports, and transforms pain—can be created.

I am very happy and content to have been able to build a great human group with excellent professionals that make up the team at Relational Home: Judit and Elisabet Deprez, Luisa Vilardell, Nancy Castrillón, Carmen Aranda, Alberto Plaza, Anna Aranda, Eva Gabarró and Claudio Moreno.

All my gratitude to my family, the cornerstone of my life. This edition is especially dedicated to Lourdes, my mother, who supported this book from the moment it was conceived. Her dedication, love, and trust gave me the wings to "fly" and overcome all the challenges I've faced throughout my life.

To my daughters: for being and for existing; for inspiring me, for moving me, and for how we have become the brave women we are today. I am proud of you, and I feel incredibly fortunate to have you and to have us. I cannot imagine a better family than ours. The adventure of motherhood has been a challenge, a continuous learning process, and an exciting experience, not without its difficulties, but all surmountable.

My close-knit family has been and continues to be my driving force and main support: my sister Silvia, my cousins, all the people who have formed it, and those who are still a part of it. I have always believed that what heals is the relationship, and without these significant and essential ones, it would have been very difficult or impossible to move forward. We are born with the neurological need to have secure attachments that provide us with emotional availability in moments of affliction, and these must remain constant from early childhood and throughout life.

When the waters of the river of life are turbulent, the best thing to do is to create a "Romanesque bridge," as my cousin Marta defines it. This bridge is not just any bridge but a relational and emotional one that allows us to move from one side to the other, protecting ourselves and preventing these waters from dragging us away and swallowing us up. I associate this bridge metaphor with the lyrics of the song "Bridge over Troubled Water" by Simon & Garfunkel, where closeness, support, and assistance to others are offered. We fight to stop being objects of others' designs and instead become agents of our own, creators of our destiny and future.

I am eternally grateful to the loyal and lifelong friends who have been there through thick and thin, supporting me in every step with boundless love and generosity, making the tough times easier; this is especially to you: Mari Ángeles Poulin and Albert Sanjuan, to Myriam Serrano, to my "magnificent Calera friends" with whom I share a tender and genuine friendship, to Ceneta for her warmth and human quality, and also for contributing ideas to the original book, to the theater group and friends from the gym. To Carina Gironella, my high school friend with whom I reconnected these past few years, and we have resumed our friendship as if no time had passed between us, still maintaining the same connection and attunement we had 30 years ago, when we were young girls. There have also been others who have been there when they could and in the way that was possible for them. Thank you all!

Nick Cross deserves a special mention for being a friend, colleague, and faithful translator of all my presentations in English. We shared hours and hours of dialogue to find the best expression and to capture my idea or concept in the best way.

On a professional level, I am very grateful to Rosa Velasco and Ramon Riera for giving me the opportunity to learn about Psychotherapy and Relational Psychoanalysis in Barcelona and for organizing meetings with significant contemporary authors. From them, especially from Rosa, I have learned to look at and listen to patients in a broader way, to immerse myself in the wonderful and little-explored world of the feeling of shame, as it seems essential to identify it in order to help patients who suffer from an arrest in their emotional development.

Later, I became a member of IARPP Spain and International (International Association for Relational Psychoanalysis and Psychotherapy) and I met other great figures of this perspective, such as Joan Coderch, Juan José Martínez, Alejandro Ávila, Carlos Rodríguez Sutil, Paco Sáinz, Catalina Munar, Rosario Castaño, Concepció Garriga, Neri Daurella, Raimundo Guerra, José González Guerras, Isabel Pérez Rigau, Mercedes Güell, Nancy Castrillón, Mari Ángeles Soler, Luisa Vilardell, Lucía Blanco, Montserrat Barragán, Aleksandra Misiolek, among many others, with whom I have shared different spaces. Catalina Munar was my supervisor for years and instilled in me the importance of tender listening, curiosity about the stories of absent parents, and the ability to understand them without judgment when their children had suffered from relational trauma, abuse, or parental neglect.

An important part of my "internal choir" is made up, first of all, by authors like Donna Orange, whose principles of humility and clinical hospitality have always guided me. Her wisdom as a philosopher, as a psychologist, and as an extraordinarily humane person makes her the very image of what authenticity, dedication to those who suffer, and absolute coherence as a subject mean to me. The list is very long, but I would like to highlight: Robert Stolorow, Andrew Morrison, Ruth Lijtmaer, Shelley Doctors, P. Bromberg, S. Mitchell, Margaret Mitchell, Hazel Ipp, Anthony Bass, D. Stern, M. Slavin, Susana Federici, Peggy Crastnopol, Sandra Buechler, André Sassenfeld, Victor Doñas, Lew Aron, Jessica Benjamin, Marie Saba, Alejandra

Plaza, Adriana Cuenca, Anne Marie Maxwell, Eyal Rozmarin, Steve Kuchuk, and especially one of the most intelligent, loyal, coherent, and genuine contemporary psychoanalysts I have ever met: Galit Atlas, who has become a dear friend. I've had the honor of sharing fascinating events with her on the legacy and intergenerational transmission of trauma. Her book *Emotional Inheritance* sheds light on the darkness of trauma and offers a comprehensive theoretical-clinical understanding of human suffering that is broad, inclusive, and hopeful, as psychotherapy opens the door to healing. Atlas describes it this way: "Although the journeys to healing vary from one person to another, they all begin with the decision to search, to open the door and approach the pain of the past instead of turning our backs on it. We decide to unravel our emotional inheritance and become active agents in transforming our destiny, taking the reins of it" (Atlas, 2022).

One of the most heartfelt thanks goes to Dr. Alberto Samperisi, a psychiatrist from San Luis (Argentina), and his dear family (Mecha, Mer, Tiziana, Gabriel, etc.), whom I consider my Argentine family. We built very strong bonds of trust and affection, and they welcomed me into their home with warmth, compassion, and generosity that I had never experienced before (with people I have just met). It was there that I made the first presentation of the book, and it was very well received. Tere Correa was my connection to the entire San Luis community, and I am very grateful for her trust and her friendship. I also want to include the tireless and resilient Jacquelina Nanclares, the always-available Silvia Saraceno, and many other colleagues who attended and participated in the book presentation at UNSL (University of San Luis).

Life has led me down paths that have brought me closer to colleagues and friends like the "super nice" and wise Yanina Piccolo and Victoria Font Saravia from IARPP Buenos Aires. We have built bridges of knowledge, an intense bond and also maintain creative collaborations, such as the workshops on OH Cards (decks composed of metaphorical cards, which are small works of art painted by artists. This is a useful therapeutic tool, as its images stimulate emotional processes that depend on the right hemisphere).

A special mention for the group of colleagues from UIC (Intercontinental University of Mexico), led by Roberto Vargas, to whom I am deeply grateful for the trust he placed in me, as well as to Claudia Villanueva, a wise, genuine, attentive, and generous woman, to the dear José Aguilar, and to Karla Escenaro. We have co-constructed very interesting and intense relational exchanges, whether it be for class planning, congress interventions, or collaborations.

On the other hand, the GRILPP (Ibero-Latin American Relational Group for Psychotherapy and Psychoanalysis) has been developing and consolidating. It was conceived by Juan José Martínez, the last president of IARPP Spain, whose recent passing has left the relational community somewhat orphaned, although we are left with all his wisdom condensed in his books. This group, which brings together and connects Latin American countries, Spain, and Portugal, is a new space for exchange, co-learning, growth, and expansion of the relational perspective.

I am also grateful to the Relational Home study and reading group, where we connect with psychologists from different countries, cultures, and life stages. This diversity does not prevent us from enriching the way we view the clinical cases we share. In this incredibly interesting and nurturing exchange space, we "cook together" with: Carmen Aranda, Montserrat Barragán, Judith Alalu,

Natalia Hanckes, María Fernanda González, Michelle Cobian, among others.

For many years, I have been actively involved in and leading the Relational Psychotherapy Working Group at COPC (Official College of Psychologists of Catalonia), a space dedicated to promoting our perspective. Two years ago, the core of the group created a very solid team: the Contemporary Psychoanalysis Working Group, formed by Ester Bonell, Carmen Aranda, Nick Cross, and Eulàlia Ruiz with other members joining over time. We believe it is important for new psychology professionals to be introduced to different perspectives, ways of working, and approaches to listening to patients where suffering is not regarded as pathology, as R. Stolorow (2015) states.

WHAT TO EXPECT FROM THIS BOOK?

Writing, that is, recording our experiences, is the healthiest and most healing therapeutic tool I have found to ease discomfort. Enduring experiences so painful that tear your soul and heart apart brings about an unbearable pain which requires great effort not to be overwhelmed by immense sadness, humiliation, anger, resentment, hatred, and the desire for revenge, among other emotions. Everything that is silenced, everything we cannot talk about, can freeze and block us, putting our life on pause. So, how do we unpause it? An unexamined and unprocessed past will not allow us to move forward, but will instead keep us as guardians of our history (Atlas, 2022). This is why it is so important to understand and free ourselves from our roots and move toward a future where we can live fully.

Mexican painter Frida Kahlo once said, "I am writing to all of you with my eyes," a powerful and graphic way of describing her art. Writing is very difficult, and conveying what you feel, and how you feel, is even harder. I hope this book is written in a way that is visually pleasant and goes much deeper, touching the reader's innermost being. I hope some may find themselves in these thoughts and feelings, embrace them as their own and ours, and have a good and therapeutic visual experience. (Without pretending to compare it to a work of art like F. Kahlo's!) It is a face-to-face confrontation with cruelty.

Identifying, recording, and transforming this pain is necessary for survival and for helping other people who are victims of abusive relationships. Emotional pain should not be considered pathological in itself, as it is part of our experiences. What could be pathological, however, is the inability to recognize or feel it. This is one of the main goals of this book. The other goal is to convey the importance of never surrendering to fear, terror, suffering, or the anger you feel when facing a hard and deadly disease like cancer.

For me, professional identity is a fundamental pillar that gives cohesion and consistency to a wounded, sometimes amputated, and annihilated "Self." When your work fulfills and satisfies you, it becomes therapeutic. Moreover, in psychotherapy sessions, we as therapists learn a lot from our patients, and we are aware of the mutual and reciprocal influence we exert on one another. To enhance our capacity for understanding, we need to learn from others *and accept their challenges.*

I fully agree with Roberto Vargas' position when he states: "As we become more aware of our existence and our vulnerability, of our fears and conflicts, we come closer to others and better understand the secrets hidden in human commitments, existential dilemmas, paradoxes, and the knots that shape relationships between people. We are better able to understand silences, glances, pauses, heartbeats, sweating, breathing, body posture, gestures, movements, facial expressions... We as psychoanalysts are sensitive to these subjective portraits, curious about this type of communication, and deeply moved when we witness the richness of human sensitivity" (Vargas, 2022).

During a therapy session, a patient asked me, "Where do you come from, Laura?" The strength of this question, his penetrating gaze, and the moment we were both in led me to answer sincerely: "I come from there." (I will elaborate more on this in the first chapter).

When the session ended, I realized that I had already emerged from the unbearable and intangible place of pain. At that moment, I became fully aware. He didn't need to ask me anything else... he knew. We both knew implicitly. This was a patient who experienced and suffered a lot of physical and emotional pain, and this intensity connected with my own extremely painful life experiences at the moment. Silently, his pain connected with mine, and the emotional connection through pain helped both of us, each in our own way, to calm, soothe, heal, and transform it.

The heartbreaking experiences of Helen (which the reader will find detailed in the second chapter), her long and dizzying journey toward freedom, crossed paths with another painful life experience of my own. We accompanied each other through the harsh processes of both abuse and cancer with an excellent emotional attunement, as she could feel that I was feeling what she was feeling. Pain needs an environment of human understanding, a relational home, a safe and hospitable space that allows us to digest and transform the traumatic experiences we have lived.

Self-revelations, experiences identified in therapeutic sessions, and taking an active role, beyond the therapeutic space, rather than being a passive spectator at a social level, created an ethical-civic commitment that I have tried to reflect in these pages.

Not silencing the atrocities and injustices endured. Not being complicit with the various "devils" that surround us in the realms of life (personal, political, economic, religious, or cultural) and confronting them fearlessly. And, above all, striving to prevent situations like those described here, and those suffered by many others who endure pain.

The American movement *"Unsilencing,"* which is now gaining momentum in the U.S. due to the political and social unrest they are experiencing, encourages, as pointed out in this book, that therapists can get involved and leave behind the role or law of silence, which has done so much harm to many individuals from previous generations and also allows to show our most human, empathetic, and connected side to the external and social reality we are all living.

PRELIMINARY COMMENT
Montserrat Barragán

Fear, pain, trauma, forgetting who you are, and forgetting your dreams should never be a place to settle in.

Pain is Deaf and its author have both nourished, enriched, and strengthened themselves over the years. It is a great honor for me, and I am extremely grateful to my friend Laura Molet for the opportunity to collaborate and join her in this new adventure: on the one hand, the updated edition of her book, as well as this English version.

I met Laura Molet at her presentation of *Pain is Deaf* at the IARPP Spain Conference in Seville in October 2019.

At that same event, I presented my work *"Whose Feeling of Hopelessness Was It?"* (Barragán 2020). Through the analysis of a clinical case, in my paper I reflect on the way in which the patient and therapist experience psychobiological feedback with each other (Coderch 2012). That is why in the treatment of patients with chronic depression, deep sadness, hopelessness, emptiness, and meaninglessness are also experienced by their therapist. "I feel that you feel what I feel" (BCPSG 2008).

Laura's presentation moved me deeply, and I felt that the way we talked about our job had enormous similarities. I had no doubt, and I approached her to thank her and congratulate her for her presentation. I wanted to have the book NOW!—to continue learning from her story and her proposal.

This book is about hope, courage, bravery, remembering your strength, believing in yourself, surrounding yourself with the people you love, going out and being free. All this, despite the fact that the core of the book deals with extremely painful and distressing issues such as trauma, violence, abuse, the enemy in the shape of cancer, or a person who pursues and threatens the deepest part of your being, promoting the reduction and crushing of the Self until you doubt whether you have been to blame for everything that happened to you.

Pain, uncertainty, and the search for a breath of fresh air to survive knows no limits of language or borders between countries. That is why, for some time now, I have joined in dreaming about the new English version and started working on it to try to contribute to giving it wings that could take *Pain is Deaf* further.

We want it to accompany more people who have suffered and who suffer, to get the message across: Yes, there can be a way out. Don't stop searching. The importance of staying close to family, friends, and colleagues. But above all, it carries a message of strength and hope.

Pain is Deaf is a sensitive and profound proposal for patients and therapists. It invites us, in an authentic and genuine way, to recognize and confront pain. On the one hand, it creates a space to think about art as a way of giving an outlet to pain, of giving it a voice so that it can be recorded, recognized, and processed. Painting, writing, music, and her reflections on them lead us by the hand to open our minds and, little by little, get to know Helen's story and struggle. Unresolved traumatic experiences can lead to chronic depression; these experiences are "buried" in the body as "embodied memories" and unconsciously determine thinking, feeling, and acting in the present. The analyst identified in the enactment and in the transference that "living in the present" of pain (Leuzinger-Bohleber 2012).

That is to say, the topics discussed in this book apply to everyone, regardless of which side you are on. It does not matter if you are a patient or a therapist. It is dedicated to people who are healthy, as well as those who are suffering from a disease as terrifying as cancer and who are going through aggressive treatments. It speaks to those who have relationships that nourish them emotionally and those who are struggling to discern which relationships would be better to leave, those who are going through grief and do not handle it well, as well as those who have more functional tools to do so.

Thanks to the evolution of psychoanalysis (for example, to intersubjective and relational thinking), the vision of our work has been enriched. Today, we understand it as two or more people—with their subjectivities—who try to understand each other and find a way out, taking into account, of course, the inevitable asymmetry in the therapeutic relationship.

The co-construction of a Relational Home (Stolorow 2007) to confront pain and trauma is the only way to give voice to sorrow, to know the enemy, and be able to look him in the face to say, "I am no longer afraid of you." Promoting confidence and hope that movements can be made against stagnation, suffering, and the repetition of scenarios that put us in the same place.

What are we therapists if not companions in search of truth, hope, freedom? What are we if not accomplices of our patients in building new paths and really getting to know themselves, to stop lying to themselves? What are we if not individuals who have taken all this as their profession, each therapist having their own battles, falls, and wounds that have not closed?

INTRODUCTION
Ruth Lijtmaer

It is an honor to have been invited by Laura to write the introduction to this book. The subject of pain is one that we all feel, whether physical or emotional. In this book Laura describes with intensity, emotion and reflection the sense of pain produced by an emotional conflict and the physical pain of suffering from cancer.

Her comparison with art, whether visual or written, shows us how the artist can express his pain in art, and we the spectators can relate to this. Talking about art made me think of music, particularly when Laura talks about the non-verbal experience and the feeling of being felt. Music being a more abstract genre, sounds allow us to connect with the joy or pain of the composer. Music is feeling, it is revolutionary, it is a universal language, it is intangible like thoughts and feelings, but it is real.

Sometimes patients find something musical in the therapist that allows them to relate more intimately, and they expect the therapist to respond to that as well. In those moments how we "sound" is the door that leads us to feel what flavor we have emotionally. Using my ideas about music, I want to emphasize how Laura listens, hears her patients in pain, and feels their pain and her own. I wonder if these interactions allow Laura to better listen and better tolerate the pain of others and her own.

Laura mentions my work on immigration. There is also pain and mourning there; pain for what was lost: homeland, family, friends, beloved objects, as well as the process of mourning, which may or may not happen, depending on whether the person is an exile or an immigrant, that is, it depends on the circumstances that lead the person to leave their homeland. They are affected by a social trauma that is not very different from individual trauma, from abuse, or from the trauma of losing a body part, which is cancer.

But when a person escapes from a country at war or from persecution, and goes to another country, which does accept them, there is hope and a better future can be imagined. If they are not accepted, they have to continue looking for someone who wants to take them in and they have to go through another mourning process that becomes more complex because the feeling of rejection becomes very strong.

Thinking about this trauma of mourning, being able to do it and think about the future is what Laura helps Helen to achieve. It allows Helen to overcome pain, anger, disappointment and so many other negative emotions, to be recognized for herself and start a new life. All this leads to testing resilience and finding freedom. This freedom is being able to find oneself and being able to live life to the fullest.

The first clinical vignette in "The Devil Wears Paul Smith" reminds me of the notion that Hanna Arendt makes of the "banality of the perverse and evil, the banality of the devil." Based on a psychological study of Eichmann, she conceives that the perverse is a consequence of the failure of the human being to be able to think, to be able to reflect on our actions and the possibility of making judgments. Referring to Eichmann, Arendt reminds us of Albert Camus' novel *The Foreigner* (1942) in which he thoughtlessly kills a man, and then has no remorse, it just "happened." One of Hanna Arendt's critics, the philosopher Alan Wolfe, in his book Political Evil: What It is and How to Combat It? (2011), explains that Arendt focused too much on who Eichmann was instead of what Eichmann did.

These comments lead us to think about the abuser and the lack of remorse for what he did. When there is remorse expressed in words, forgiveness becomes easier and allows for reparation. When there is no remorse, it is more difficult to complete mourning. All of this is related to the crime of silence, of being able to witness and act on it. Justice is created by people making reparation, which in turn allows for integration.

Many traumatized people do not talk about their trauma experiences because as Laub & Auerhahn (1989) said, that state cannot be represented or formulated; it is often transformed into psychological or physical symptoms.

Bromberg's (2006) concept of dissociation, which he calls expected dissociation, is a conscious and adaptive mechanism for handling painful experiences, and is not pathological, but a way of surviving. Perhaps Helen used it at the beginning to continue living.

Helen's life was made up of very painful moments until she broke free; But before this, the devil and the "devil tumor" traumatized her life. She was and was not a victim of both. She fought and came through. The victim-victimized dynamic reminds me of Wachtel (2014) who says that the internal world is genuinely dynamic, fluctuating and constantly reconstituting itself in response to everyday life experiences, while simultaneously "shaping" those daily experiences through a repeated pattern of reciprocal bidirectional causality.

It is not clear to me why Helen fell into the devil's trap, other than through seduction. Readers understand that our impact on others happens not only because the way others experience us affects what our lives are like, but because the very nature of the internal world is built in the ongoing dialectic between our already existing inclinations, desires, fears, and representations (our persistent psychological structure) and the structures and inclinations that are produced and continually maintained or changed according to life experiences. At this point, again, the influences are simultaneous and bidirectional.

Another association is the article "Confusion of tongues between adults and the child" by S. Ferenczi: besides speaking of "tender" love, tenderness of the child towards the adult, which the adult understands as a sexual love, he speaks of trauma. He tells us: "What is traumatic is the unforeseen, the unfathomable, the incalculable. Unexpected, external threat, the sense of which one cannot fathom is unbearable" (p. 239). There are two important elements here: one that trauma is incomprehensible and the other that it comes without warning, unexpectedly; until this moment the person is not prepared, is not defended and feels insecure.

We have our voices to defend ourselves and our patients and not become victims of the power of men. I think it helps to remind us that walls or ramparts surrounding cities are an extension of home, identity, differentiation of the Self and the other, and of course "self-protection." These walls are also a part of the history of the world, along with racism and xenophobia, greed and power. Power includes or excludes others in order to dominate and denigrate. We cannot remain silent (Lijtmaer, 2018).

With Laura and her relationship with her, Helen conquered her liberation that allowed her an integration of the Self with the external world. It allowed her to be more prepared for an unknown and uncontrollable future, but a safer, healthier and better future for herself, being free and turning away from the devil.

This gave her serenity and strength to live life to the fullest.

I.

PAIN IS DEAF: *The Art of Transforming Pain and the Pain Transformed into Art*

"Where do you come from, Laura?" a traumatized adult patient asked me, fixing his excited and penetrating gaze into my eyes. In a moment of meeting, he felt that I was sharing in his emotional experience. It was a new experience for both of us, making a profound impact on us.

"I come from there," I responded, shocked.

My personal painful experience, my emotional tsunami (Bromberg, 2009), allowed me to connect deeply and intensely with my patient's experience of devastation and abuse, as well as with Helen, the patient I will discuss in the next chapter. From *"Working the Implicit"* (Molet, 2012), through *"Dare to Be"* (Molet, 2013), and continuing with *"Breaking the Pathological Accommodation System"* I and II (Molet, 2013-2014), I had been writing, beyond the explicit, about a traumatized adult patient, about myself, and my long way to freedom. This specific patient's experience could be registered, lived, and understood in the session because he knew and felt that I had been there.

Art has a similar effect of accompaniment and repair. Mark Rothko put it this way: "A painting is not a photo of an experience: it is the experience." A session is not only a recount of the patient's experience; it is a new experience for both the patient and the analyst. I feel that artists and relational psychoanalysts are on the same page, in the same register. Jackson Pollock said, "Painting is a self-discovery; every good artist paints what he is." We might say that each session is also a self-discovery, in which our patients uncover who they truly are, rediscovering themselves through the process of deconstructing and reconstructing their sense of self. We join them as copilots on this new journey that begins with their first consultation.

Magritte's painting "The Acrobat's Exercises" (1928) deeply captivated me. I imagined this as a possible framework for grief. Artists express experiences without formulating them (Stern, 1997), using images that capture and impact us without words. They make records of their experiences unconsciously, which can save many from madness and dissociation.

Before I knew the painting's name, I automatically thought, "Love hurts and injures," associating it with abusive relationships. When Virginia Goldner (2004) speaks about women who are victims of abuse, she says: *they can easily become us*; I was "us-them" and then I became "us" again. I am in a position to confirm that as therapists, we witness injustices that must be named to dignify the suffering endured alone and without social recognition.

Feeling recognized and resignified in essential aspects of the experiences of patient-analyst-artists have been unique therapeutic moments of mutual recognition of shared pain. This allows the patient to access feelings previously dissociated and silenced (Molet, 2014). For me, this painting suggested both elasticity, flexibility, and adaptation, as well as fragmentation of the self, chaos, pain, annihilation, submission, humiliation, and loss of integrity. Magritte was a painter of ideas and visible thoughts, revealing the continuous visibility of the invisible, in other words—beyond words and content—we are talking about implicit relational knowledge. Art should teach us that we have not really seen what we are seeing. Our work as analysts also involves co-constructing with our patients a small-great work of art, pointing out what they have not yet seen, but at the same time they do—implicitly—in a genuine and authentic exploration of the patient's vicissitudes and those that belong to the dyad itself. I believe relational therapists facilitate the creative dimension to enhance the giving-meaning process. Intersubjectivity is a kind of sensitivity, and emotional understanding requires establishing a dialogue with the patient to achieve emotional knowledge.

Those of us who are aware of the huge problem that silencing crime represents, and do not want to continue silencing or be accomplice in muteness and silence because each experience has already had to be lived in solitude and silence, we seek to dignify this suffering that had to be endured alone.

Pain is deaf—you cannot stop hearing it—and it must be integrated and connected with the person who was and used to be, to prevent the sense of self from being broken. The person who will emerge will be able to do so by assuming the pain and vulnerability of the person who was and used to be; the resulting person will be, without dissociation, who they were and who they are now, after recovering from the emotional tsunami resulting from a traumatic experience.

We can restore and work on it, ensuring that the thread connecting the past, present, and future is not broken or lost. We can disrupt the loop of incessant repetition, ensuring that the past remains past and does not interfere with the present, and that the future retains its meaning. Without this, a person lives in an alternate reality, perceiving the world as disconnected from their pain, feeling alienated and estranged, and experiencing a sense of loneliness and unbearably painful orphanhood (Carr, 2011).

The painful words of scientist Madame Curie can help us go deeper into the topic of pain: "At times it seems to me that my pain weakens and numbs, but it quickly reemerges tenacious and powerful." She lived in constant struggle against the pain of grief and became addicted to work (Montero, 2013). Frida Kahlo's artwork revolves around her biography, her own pain, and suffering: "Painting has filled my life. I have lost three children and a number of things that could have filled my horrible life. Painting has replaced everything. I believe there is nothing better than work." She also expressed, "I have been able to find a personal way to express myself in painting, without being pushed by any prejudice" (Kahlo, *Philosophizing and Painting*). Salvador Dalí was a person dominated by feelings of shame so sharp, tenacious, and painful that they almost "made his life impossible, and he could only cope by expressing them in his work, creating an exhibitionist mask to try to hide them". "Painting was an instrument, a language for recovering lost experiences; unbearable experiences are manifested, and through painting, they generate a 'soft anguish" (Riera, 2004).

A quote from the book *The Last Encounter* by Sándor Márai states: "The education he carried in his blood, which came from the forests of Paris, from the sickly sensitivity of his mother, made him unable to talk about what troubled him but had to endure it in silence. He had learned that the smartest thing to do was to stay silent. But he could not live without affection. He needed to pour his affection into someone: Nini or Konrad. Then his fever would subside, he would stop coughing, and his pale, thin face would flush with the warmth of enthusiasm and trust" (Márai, 1999).

Most of our patients would share this vital experience so meticulously described by Márai: they have learned from a very young age that it is best not to ask for help from their parental figures, not to trust anyone, that they have to manage alone, that it is "better" or "smarter," according to Márai, to remain silent, guided by an insecure attachment bond—whether avoidant (denying) or ambivalent (anxious)—because they have learned that the response from their parental figures would not contain or calm their anxiety. Nevertheless, as human beings, we cannot live without affection; otherwise, we become ill, just as happens to the protagonist in "The Last Encounter," where pain deafens the apparent silence. This is a good example of how the body can play a role in expressing painful and conflicting emotional experiences, or how somatic manifestations of overwhelming emotional experiences emerge that have not been metabolized (Doctors, 2013; Molet, 2013), causing pain and/or suffering.

We need to have learned to translate our somatic sensations into feelings that can be expressed and used for self-management and self-regulation. If there has been a relational and emotional deficit, it can be learned in the course of therapy, as development occurs in the relationship, and it is the new attachment relationship with the therapist that allows the patient to change. We create a relational home (Stolorow, 2013) of understanding where there once was orphanhood and a sense of loneliness. Interaction, relationship, and context are fundamental pillars for framing, understanding, and comprehending the subject; Wassily Kandinsky (1979), in his book *Concerning the Spiritual in Art,* already reflected on relational terms: "Any artistic creation is the child of its time, and the mother of our own feelings." Individuals and art cannot be understood without considering their intersubjective systems.

We repair deficit experiences; deficit is always a lack of registration, an experience that has not been formulated. Mental pain has to do with what has not been articulated; it is what goes unexpressed and transforms into a symptom. Suffering does express itself. In dissociation, we are unable to grasp how things affect ourselves and cannot become aware of what has impacted ourselves. Traumatic experiences induce dissociation, the multiple states of the Self of the mind, countertransference of trauma, and the self-care of the therapist (Itzkowitz, 2018).

The testimonial function of the therapeutic relationship is crucial for the reintegration of the traumatized person and for overcoming the extremes of dissociation. The true witness is one who endures being a witness (Orange, 2005). Shared pain is a pain that transforms and diminishes itself; we frame and register the patient's pain, with words, emotional connection, and understanding, instead of using the painter's brush or the written language of writers.

The therapist must be able to tolerate and hold mental pain, both their own and the patients', to be able to help in the process of transforming pain into suffering. It is neither necessary nor desirable to put ourselves in parentheses in any type of relationship, whether personal, as in the case of Helen, or professional. Holding our subjectivity, relating equitably, tolerating our vulnerability, treating ourselves and the other in a gentle way, that is, with internal coherence and cohesion, creating space for two, without the need to dominate or be dominated, with the commitment to always seek emotional understanding—our own, the patient's, and others'— trying to improve our perception by listening with a second ear: "We should find a way to listen —a way that informs us of something" (Orange, 2016).

We offer to our patients the "non-verbal experience," the experience of "feeling felt," which is crucial in the process of building a good and healthy therapeutic relationship, just as occurred with the patient whose question initiated this work; in this way, the patient can begin to integrate those experiences that had to remain dissociated because in the past they threatened a bond necessary for survival.

Human beings have various languages to transform suffering into creation: musical, literary, and/or artistic, like the artists I mentioned at the beginning of this presentation—Madame Curie, Frida Kahlo, Dalí, and S. Márai, just to quote a few examples of "universal pain." Agnes Martin, the Canadian abstract expressionist artist, who used what was called silent painting and employed her profession as therapy to counteract the psychosis she suffered, giving a spiritual dimension to her minimalist work, expressed such beautiful, sincere, and true ideas as this: "If you live anchored in the past, you will not know beauty or happiness, and in fact, you will not live." Art is the concrete representation of our most imperceptible feelings. It is a poetic way of defining and expressing the same thing when we identify a halt in the emotional development of the patient, knowing that the past interferes with their present, causing them suffering, and they do not know beauty or happiness. They actually live without living in peace and tranquility.

We practice psychoanalysis in a manner that is genuinely personal but also responsible and rigorous, as Mitchell posited, and that is how each of us conceives our own way of using the analytic process to understand the patient, helping them transform their suffering and/or pain with our commitment and effort, with our full attention (Wallin, 2006), with a spirit of inquiry, perseverance, courage, humility, resilience, feeling our vulnerability, tolerating feelings of shame, infinite responsibility toward the unknown sufferer, *hermeneutic of trust,* comprehending, acknowledging our limits and errors, avoiding reductionism and simplifications that nullify the subjectivity of the person, tuning in with the other by immersing ourselves in their internal world, with a compassionate attitude toward the suffering of another. Compassion, understood as the desire for others to be free from suffering, is a process composed of three parts: 1. Affective part: "I feel what you feel." 2. Cognitive part: "I understand you." And 3. Motivational part: "I want to help you" (Simón, 2017)—a dialogical style that is non-authoritarian, creating a space for two, restoring the dignity of profoundly devastated, wounded, humiliated, and vulnerable individuals just like ourselves.

Conclusion

The spaces for transforming pain and suffering are co-created not only in our consultations with each of our patients but also take place in museums, in front of works of art when we enter and connect with the enchanting world of beauty as a way to counteract and transform the non-beautiful, pain, and horror; a space for two is created. Just as artists use various languages to transform their pain into creation, we, the spectators, can observe and admire their works as therapy to counteract our discomfort; the silence of painting and sculpture speaks to us, moves us, and makes us feel alive. A relational and intersubjective quote from the French painter and sculptor Marcel Duchamp, creator of the Readymade, emphasizing mutual and reciprocal influence will serve to conclude this section: "The creative act is not developed solely by the artist. The viewer translates the work in contact with the external world, deciphering and interpreting its internal qualifications, and this adds their contribution to the creative act."

2.

THE DEVIL WEARS PAUL SMITH[1]

This chapter revolves around a clinical case that encapsulates and describes all the concepts presented and defined throughout this book: pain, suffering, fear, injustice, freedom, emotional tsunami, and more. It tells the story of a fifty-year-old woman who experienced profound personal upheaval. Her decision to set boundaries with a narcissistic, authoritarian husband— "When I give an order, it is executed"—resulted in significant repercussions. Her husband was financially powerful, paranoid, distrustful, and jealous, always suspecting that Helen would be *unfaithful,* whether at work or at the gym. When Helen chose to leave her gilded cage rather than remain a prisoner of marital dictatorship, she sacrificed her financial security. Her situation was further worsened by judicial ineffectiveness, as the judge accepted all the lies from her then-husband. She faced a pervasive fear instilled in her by this man, who threatened: "If you leave me, I will leave you with nothing. With me, everything—without me, nothing!"

Helen's struggle to execute her decision, confront her paralyzing fear, and challenge the terror of these violent words led her to

---

1 Paul Smith is a renowned British fashion designer. In one session, Helen associated the phrase "The Devil Wears Paul Smith" with the title of the film "The Devil Wears Prada." There is no intention to question the brands or interfere with their esteemed image; it is simply a play on words.

redefine what "without anything" could mean. Transforming her fear into new, more self-empowering forms, she moved through feelings of rage, hate, and resentment to reach a self-formulated certainty: with you dead—without you, alive. She recognized that the man she married 25 years ago no longer existed; he was referred to only by his last name, a name he claimed his family had sold to the devil for money. Now the devil was wearing Paul Smith—predatory, intelligent, arrogant, and seemingly self-sufficient, with malice and hatred that demanded an incalculable price.

The devil's seduction was his disguise, masking his feelings of inferiority and unbearable humiliation. Helen understood that his attempts to control and belittle her were rooted in his own emotional deficiencies and early emotional trauma, which he could not integrate or feel. His lack of genuine emotion left him only capable of experiencing fear, rage, anger, pain, and hate, instead of being able to access the genuine emotions at the core of his vulnerability.

Society must decide whether to remove this disguise, support it, or reflect on its role. How long will we remain passive observers of others' suffering? If we can identify the many faces of evil, why don't we act to neutralize and stop it? How can we help oppressed individuals assert themselves and fight for equality? Information alone is insufficient to recognize when one is in an abusive relationship, especially when the abuser is a skilled seducer who needs to control to exist. Silence only compounds the issue, and social media has provided a platform for testimonies and movements like #MeToo. This book aims to reach those who feel oppressed and do not know how to fight or seek help, showing that there is a way out of pain and barbarity. Until we achieve the main goal of the book—to stop being passive spectators, to refuse to silence suffering, and to demand justice and equality—I will continue to advocate for these changes.

2.1. Individual Trauma

2.1.a. The Different Faces of Evil.

Evil manifests in various forms. Guerra's (2018) book provides a framework for identifying these multiple faces of evil:

Destroying individuals or lives.

Limiting or depriving others of resources necessary for their fulfillment, without a vital need to do so.

Treating others as objects, using them to gratify one's own narcissism.

Legally oppressing and economically exploiting others in institutional contexts.

Seducing others—not only sexually—to get them to do, think, or desire things that are harmful to them. This is the visible face of evil exhibited by Helen's ex-husband and many others who exploit their partners or employees.

Using intimidation and fear to force others into submission.

Manipulating information to influence others and conform them to harmful ideologies.

Defaming and discrediting others.

Inducing unwarranted depressive states and irritation in others for selfish gratification.

During this period, Helen began to write. She used writing to soothe her pain, similar to how Frida Kahlo painted to survive her suffering or Madame Curie immersed herself in work. Helen wrote to understand and transform her suffering and to give voice to her experiences. She was determined to break the family relational pattern of silence, understanding that silence was an ally of deaf pain. She believed it was more beneficial for these experiences to be heard and read by those who would listen.

Writing helped her connect with her pain, empathize more broadly, and apply new insights to her life, profession, and activism. It allowed her to adopt an altruistic stance, avoid victimhood, and reject passivity. Therapy enabled her to confront and understand her experiences, integrate her identity, and transform her suffering. She realized that running away from problems or denying them was not a solution, nor was resorting to alcohol or addictive relationships. While a positive attitude is important, it should not invalidate one's pain or deny reality. This false optimism, often promoted by self-help and positive psychology, is akin to "Fast Food-Fast Happiness."

2.1.b. Helen and Cancer

Helen faced a setback with an unexpected diagnosis: breast cancer. The pain was no longer muted. The cancer in her left breast was described as a nest, symbolizing home and family. She felt it deeply; the tumor represented the culmination of her struggles. Helen hoped that, after its removal, she would experience a new beginning. Before the surgery, she visualized the doctor not only removing the tumor but also extracting the suffering accumulated over the past five terrible years. She imagined the residual pain—humiliation, rage, sadness, fear, terror, hopelessness, injustice, anger, impotence—being expelled, leaving her feeling completely and truly free, unshackled from the chains of anger.

The pain and suffering had condensed in her left breast as a final consequence of the traumatic experience. With her therapist, she coined the term "Tumorized Emotional Tsunami" (TET), inspired by Molet (2017-18), to describe the enduring impact of the trauma on both emotional and physical levels. Such deep, heartbreaking trauma can leave physical scars, like a tumor, in the core of one's being.

From this point, Helen embarked on a journey of renewal— emotionally, relationally, and physically. She faced the physical changes of chemotherapy, including a haircut and shaving her head, with dignity, courage, and bravery. This transformation was both encouraging and frightening. Would she be able to endure it?

She reminded herself, "If I have not been submissive to the devil, I will not be submissive to pain or resign myself to the disease." This rebellion was driven by visible causes: a body wounded by trauma and injustice. Frida Kahlo's paintings, portraying herself with all her pain, pierced by steel and corsets, provided comfort, symbolizing a fighter against a cruel reality. Helen, however, disagreed with accepting her body as an infernal prison; she believed it should no longer be a prison now that she was no longer in the golden cage with the devil.

Helen thought of Stolorow's concept that trauma ends through time, finding solace in the belief that cancer might end her trauma. She hoped to break the vicious cycle and repetitive loop of traumatic temporality. One loop she wanted to break was the automatic guilt she felt about everything, a tactic her psychologically abusive ex-husband used to torment her. She refused to feel guilty for having cancer or to view herself as a victim. This cycle ended with the tumor and the surgeon's removal.

Manipulators, harassers, and pathological narcissists often use their power to manipulate and harm others, leading to deep trauma. Helen's ex-husband had tried to deplete and destroy her, using her to overcome his own miseries and feelings of inferiority. He failed to accept that Helen had had enough. When something is over, it's simply over, but accepting this is a challenge, especially for someone like him. Helen was initially filled with rage, humiliation, and resentment, but she eventually found strength, dignity, and vitality to emerge from this difficult place.

She wanted to embrace and believe in the submissive woman she had been, thanks to therapeutic support. She moved from a defenseless position to a "defense mode," confronting her fears without shame. Her only fear was the tumor itself, which she faced with resolve. She did not fear the physical limitations or side effects of her treatment; instead, she endured them with stoic bravery and strength.

Helen's ability to protect herself from de-idealization and her newfound sense of freedom enriched her. She chose to leave psychological bankruptcy behind and embrace a real bankruptcy, shifting from "With me everything, without me nothing" to "With you nothing, without you everything." The integration of her Self, previously fragmented, gave her the internal coherence and strength needed to move forward. She was determined not to let anyone—neither the devil, the tumor, nor chemotherapy—take away her voice or her fight for personal freedom. Her struggle was her power, her way of living in the world with a renewed sense of vindication.

Facing chemotherapy and its consequences, Helen understood the importance of attitude. From integrative medicine to common sense, maintaining a positive attitude, with strength, humor, and surrounded by love, significantly improves one's experience. Contrary to common advice to "learn to be a chronic patient" or "get used to feeling bad," Helen found it more meaningful to relate to cancer and its effects rather than submit to them. This approach gave her the confidence to face her illness, except for the eighth session, when she felt extremely unwell.

Helen described the eighth chemo session: «I felt the liquid going into my body slowly, as usual; but I was angrier than ever. I felt dizzy, disgusted, and repugnance. When I got home, I realized I had read disturbing news about the verdict on 'the pack' and various opinions on rape, Use, Ab - use. . . », Helen was particularly sensitive to issues of rape, having been affected by a similar case in her family when she was young, (when she was 13 years old, her cousin was raped and the "law of silence" was imposed on the family, with the consequences that this had for all the cousins, and for herself, since not being able to talk about fear and pain was very traumatic). She is very sensitive to injustice as well, especially when perpetrated by a judge. That kind of scenario made her sick to her stomach. A judge holds excessive power: and if the judge is a sexist, misogynist man, he will not be fit (because he will not be impartial) to issue rulings, as he leaves a large portion of the population in absolute defenselessness. That's why that night she had a horrible nightmare: she dreamt of the judge who sided with the devil, who silenced— and was complicit in—every lie of her ex-husband, who didn't read (and rejected them "because they don't proceed") any of her pieces of evidence that demonstrated and dismantled each of the devil's miserable lies; the judge let himself be seduced by the devil, another man who doesn't love women (Larsson, 2005); for a judge to issue rulings that could ruin your life is very dangerous, and for everyone to side with the one who has economic power is frustrating... Is this what we call justice? What is the rule of law? Who has the right to what? How much defenselessness and frustration to self-regulate and manage.

Economic power is not synonymous with being a person of power, since they are poor and vile in important matters like the richness of feelings and emotional nuances. The power to possess something—wealth, or someone without their consent—must be "very powerful" and make you feel that way. Helen became once again aware of the importance of trauma, of the shadow of the tsunami that follows you throughout life when news cross your path, reminding you of where you come from, of your traumatic experience, and you know that the shadow of the tsunami is long and stretches far...

If something ends in our lives, it's for our evolution, so it's better to let it go, move forward, and grow enriched by our good or bad experiences.

"Trauma ends with time (...) Trauma breaks the ordinary unity and linearity of temporality in a devastating way. (...) The past becomes present, the future loses any meaning other than that of endless repetition" (Stolorow, 2012).

What role does "the infinity of the unsaid," and "the unformulated experience"—terms coined by D. Stern (2021)—play in all of this?

This can help us understand much of the therapeutic process carried out by Helen; these concepts can be applied both to verbal and non-verbal aspects. To formulate contents, create them, or make them meaningful. Emotionally forbidden contents, but cognitively feasible. They are part of the potential experience that remains in an unformulated state for unconscious defensive reasons, that is, dissociated. Formulation is understood as an episode of *insight*. To formulate an experience is to give it meaning. What is the dividing line between formulated and unformulated experience? A change in the interpersonal field makes it possible for participants to formulate an experience that until then had not been formulated: when a new meaning emerges, it is because one can now tolerate or accept something that could not be tolerated or accepted before. The NON-SELF becomes SELF. The subjectivity that had been unformulated, insignificant, dissociated, not I and not Self, becomes formulated, meaningful, "I," and part of the Self. This is why I said that this concept is very important to understand Helen's healing process, her process of change, and our moments of meeting, as they allowed her to unlock her initiative and make a risky but courageous decision.

With a cohesion and consistency of herself never felt before, thanks to the fact that she was able to formulate her entire experience, she stopped being dissociated from herself and could integrate it into her Self, leaving free mental space. Human beings need to register emotional experiences to free up space in our minds so that new experiences can enter. We learn from experiences and from others. Embracing suffering is a natural way to transform it into pain; for this, it is essential to share it with someone sensitive. A healthy mourning is always done in company. A sorrow that cannot be cried out leaves a scar on the person who endures it.

This beautiful poem about *scars* was shared with me by a patient, and I find it perfect to give it a space between these lines. It goes like this:

"There is no scar, no matter how brutal it may seem,
that doesn't hold beauty.
A specific story is told in it,
some pain. But also its end.

Scars, then, are the seams of memory.
An imperfect finish that heals us
by hurting us. The way time finds
so that we never forget the wounds."

Any flagrant violation of human rights and freedom is devastating. It is an attack. And it is condemnable. To know and be complicit in a traumatic experience and silence it is a crime and an attack. And it should be condemnable. The systematic use of violence to achieve objectives, whether political, personal, economic, social, or religious-cultural, is an attack. And it is also condemnable. It creates insecurity, anguish, humiliation, impotence, rage, fear, terror, pain, shame, devastation, and sometimes, an amputation of the Self. In the U.S., as I mentioned earlier, there are campaigns and groups focused on relational and intersubjective psychology that are organizing conferences and talks to stop silencing, or *unsilencing*, confronting all that we are not talking about, the ways in which doing nothing can be complicity and, therefore, dangerous; it invites us to consider the margins between what is said, what we wish to avoid speaking about, and what cannot be verbalized. Reflecting on how we silence ourselves, and whether we wish to do so, is the beginning of positive change on a social level, with more involvement from us as therapists and those who understand very traumatic, unjust, and sometimes, heartbreaking stories. This proposal is also present in these pages.

We must be brave to live with fear. It takes a lot of courage to face fear, pain, injustice, barbarity, meaninglessness, madness.... Being afraid of terror, terrorist and abusive acts, and illnesses is normal, healthy, and legitimate.

Let us not be ashamed to admit that we have had, or have, fear; it is an emotion that we can transform, as long as we do not dissociate or deny it.

The terrifying acts committed by terrorists and the terrifying acts committed by abusers have a great and ominous parallel: feelings and sensations shared by those who are victims of them. These two phenomena are part of social and collective trauma, and they create a great deal of uncertainty that is difficult to manage.

2.2. The Social trauma (*The trauma of which we are witnesses): The pack, Immigration, exiles.*

Ruth Lijtmaer is the colleague and friend who has made me most sensitive and made me reflect on social Trauma, immigration-exiles-deportations; on what immigrants feel, emigrating to another land is a complex psychosocial situation, which involves countless losses with a profound impact on each subject; it is a loss of contextual continuity (Lijtmaer, 2017). There is a qualitative and quantitative difference between the experience of being an emigrant, an exile or a refugee; in the latter cases there is political, religious or ethnic persecution and they are people who flee to save their lives and those of their families. This means that they have to leave quickly, without time to prepare and mentalize themselves. In addition, they are treated as non-humans, and suffer a feeling of abandonment, dehumanization, loss of identity and integrity, helplessness, frustration, anger and fear, since nobody wants them. They live in a state of "homelessness." They have no home. They live in a world without meaning. Their status will depend on the conditions imposed by their host country.

There is a distortion of the sense of time and space (Lijtmaer, 2017).

The long road to freedom is one that allows people who suffer from it to remove the chains that bind them to hatred, resentment, and thirst for revenge, and through which they can access the status or state of being a free person. Truly free: without bombs, without being subjected to an abuser, free of malignant tumors, and feeling that they have the possibility of being themselves, without having the obligation to be who others want them to be, or to think that they have to do or say what they think their husband wants them to do or say, even if they don't think so. The heavy imperative that was overriding Helen: "When I give an order, it is executed" was slowly dissipating, as she stopped feeling subject to the orders and desires of her ex.

Success in intervening in abusive relationships lies in part in trying to make love safer for women and less threatening for men. Vulnerable men who depend on their women and appear to be autonomous, strong, independent. The narcissistic fragility of these men leads them to transform any painful affection into anger; *ceasing to protect and justify* a person you love, but who hurts you, can be as dangerous for you as if a terrorist wanted you to self-immolate. Gathering the strength, the courage, the bravery, to dare to be yourself and to rescue yourself from death and an annulment of your subjectivity and try to carefully remove the bomb belt, trying not to let it explode in the attempt, thinking that this task is more than legitimate, although your pulse trembles from the panic and terror you feel.... And the Trembling, insecurity, and hesitation are not good for deactivating bombs. What is the way out? How to regulate and manage a situation of maximum stress? Therapeutic help to find healthy tools and resources, and meaningful support is a good solution to deactivate the bomb. Don't let it explode! Another solution is to become aware of the value and crime of silence. No more abuse, no more consent to it, not Helen, nor anyone else in her place. For this we need to be able to speak, speak with a calm, clear, concrete and concise voice and say: Enough is enough!!! In this section on abusive relationships, I am not only referring to the case of Helen: a man abuses a woman, but I would like to have, and I would also invite readers to have, a broader and more extensive view, and apply it to any other relationship of abuse of power, such as the case of those persecuted and exiled for political, cultural, religious, ethnic reasons... cases of mistreatment at school or bullying, cases of mobbing, etc. We must endure being a witness to great and small injustices in order to name and dignify a suffering that we bear alone, in silence and without social recognition. We must give voice to this solitary and silent suffering and try to make the shared pain no longer deaf and mute.

Social and cultural recognition is necessary to dignify people who suffer and to give them validation, support and assistance. And also so that society stops being a silent accomplice to abuse and injustice.

The true witness is the one who can bear it (Orange, 2005). Shared pain and fear is what can be transformed; we record the patient's pain by putting it into words, with connection and emotional understanding. We offer patients non-verbal experience, the experience of *feeling felt* "I feel that you feel what I feel", which is fundamental for a good and healthy therapeutic relationship. In this way, patients can integrate experiences that they have had to dissociate because they felt their parental bond and connection necessary for survival was threatened, breaking the system of pathological accommodation (Molet, 2013–2014). We have a voice and the opportunity to give voice to our patients; in this current society, therapists are not as neutral as before, nor are we alien to human pain. We join voices to fight. Voices to dignify ourselves. Voices to denounce and to be able to say Stop!!! At the IARPP international congress held in June of 2018 in New York, the active and useful role we have at a social level was discussed, beyond the individual or group role of each clinical case. Opening paths of hope, compassion, creating organizations....

Together we can do things to avoid being passive witnesses. In this reality, which sometimes seems like fiction or a movie, we all appear with more or less leading roles. And sometimes the roles can change, or be exchanged, you can be a victim and a therapist at the same time, or one of the two, or neither. Let us not forget that *they* (victims of brutal attacks) can be us, and that *they* (perpetrators) can also be us. Do we feel calm and with a good conscience if we are only spectators? And let us not forget to ask ourselves: Why does someone dress up as a devil? Why is seduction not only allowed, but also well regarded and promoted on social media and in society in general? Liquid society and society of emotional deprivation, of immediate gratification, of lack of commitment, of insecurity and fear of feeling and expressing....

Idealization- de-idealization of romantic love: one of the most common ways of seeking refuge from pain is through the supposed gratification that a romantic relationship is believed to provide... usually with high expectations, and with the mistaken conviction that it will be their "other half," their complement, leading to toxic or unhealthy ways of constructing a partnership; expecting the other to fulfill one's subjective needs is a serious and frequent mistake; in the initial phase of idealization and infatuation, there is hope that this will be the case. As the relationship progresses, mutual reproaches and blame emerge, as well as the desire to change the other person to be and act as one had desired, and to pathologically adjust and conform to what the other person wants. The success of a healthy relationship lies precisely in the opposite: mutual respect and recognition of one another, with a reciprocal and mutual influence without either person ceasing to be themselves. Neither submitting nor being submitted. An equitable relationship. Fitting together. The thirdness (Benjamin, 1988), that is, a space created by both, is the best antidote to toxic relationships.

CONCLUSIONS

I would feel satisfied if my efforts give voice to the painful, lonely, and silent suffering experienced by many victims of traumatic situations. My aim has been to make this pain no longer be deaf, invisible, and mute, to provide it with a place and social recognition. Such recognition is essential for those who suffer to feel valued.

I feel this is an invitation to readers, as Galit Atlas suggests, to explore new perspectives on trauma, creativity, suffering, and transformation. We transform by analyzing and verbalizing abuse, remorse, reparation, and the healing process.

As Ruth Lijtmaer rightly emphasizes in the introduction, echoing the phrase of the banality of the devil, remorse and forgiveness are critical in the process of mourning, pain, and repair. She notes: "When there is remorse expressed in words, forgiveness becomes easier and allows for repair." However, what happens when there is neither forgiveness nor remorse, but the opposite? In a Kafkian incredulity moment, when Helen asked her ex-husband, why he had lied so much, he responded, "It's the price you have to pay for wanting to get a separation." Those words were not reparative; they were like bloody daggers piercing her pain. Then, it was clear that she was going to fight to get out of there, with her effort, vitality, dignity, and as a human rights activist, she wanted to put words to pain, to repair, to injustice, and to the possibility of escaping the place of human waste, the human sewer. ("You'll end up like a filthy sewer rat!" A stone-cold, legendary, and unfortunate threat he angrily dedicated to Helen.) And there is a way out. It's very hard, but it is achieved. Transmitting courage to people who suffer, as Donna Orange (2013) divinely points out.

Regarding the complex issue of forgiveness, I agree with Claudia Villanueva's opinion: "At first, I want to emphasize that the ability to forgive and the exercise of forgiveness are subjective experiences that involve great elaboration and are very difficult to carry out and, for this reason, they cannot be considered or embraced as if they were simple psychological achievements or as something that only concerns the individual's will, as sometimes appears in religious discourse or in the literature of certain therapies. Rather, I consider them to be subjective experiences whose development and culmination can be favored under certain conditions. The ability to forgive is supported by the experience of having grown up in a context that allowed the processing of certain feelings that initially seemed intolerable, such as pain, anger, or rage arising from harm received or intense frustration. If caregivers embrace and tolerate these feelings themselves, then the child will have the opportunity to process them, which would prevent them from becoming entrenched, and thus, they can emerge in the horizon of emotional possibilities. As adults, this ability would also be supported by the ability to see the offender in a broad context that includes both the conditions of their development and their situation at the moment of committing the offense." (Villanueva, C).

We know, as Ruth Lijtmaer has pointed out, that if the offender denies their responsibility, shows no remorse, and makes no attempts to repair the harm, the victim will find it much harder to free themselves from bitterness, resentment, and desires for revenge. Following Claudia Villanueva's quote: "In such circumstances, processing the offense and abandoning the feelings I just mentioned in order to repair the relationship seems unlikely and, possibly, undesirable. Forgiveness can be defined as the renunciation of resentment, hatred, anger, and the desire for revenge toward those who have done something serious that would justify those responses, at least in the subjective register of the offended. But we may ask ourselves: Is forgiveness the best and healthiest response to the offense? Are all offenses and harms forgivable? Can one forgive someone who never acknowledged their wrongdoing?"

I agree with Claudia that it is possible to overcome bitterness, resentment, and the desire for revenge, without this implying the restoration of the relationship. In fact, holding on to resentment, hatred, and the desire for revenge is a way of perpetuating the bond with the aggressor, as Searles (cited by Lansky, 2008) points out. Overcoming these feelings is what allows for the dissolution of the harmful bond and opens up the possibility for other alternatives. In this case, following the same article, the person would forgive in the sense of overcoming bitterness and resentment and would do so motivated more by the desire or need to restore their own emotional health and peace of mind, but would not forgive in the sense of restoring the relationship. Instead, they would choose to distance themselves, put the memory at a distance, detach from the image of the offender, and attempt to rebuild their life by leaving all of that behind. Helen's clinical case exemplifies this position and this solution as the one most considerate of herself and the most reparative.

It seems wise for therapists to reflect on the proposal that a good therapeutic process necessarily includes forgiveness in the sense of restoring the bond and reconciling with the offender as a therapeutic goal. I also agree with Claudia, regarding the idea that any form of psychotherapy that assumes that only through the ability to forgive and exercise forgiveness can resentment and bitterness be overcome, might paradoxically, be retraumatizing for some people. It is vital to help the patient overcome resentment, bitterness, and the desire for revenge, especially because these feelings can be very damaging to themselves (in fact, in Helen's case, she feels that the cancerous tumor condensed much unprocessed pain: resentment, anger, and frustration that she couldn't metabolize due to the overwhelming intensity, because it was almost ungraspable), but we must always understand that it is an inalienable right of the patient whether to forgive or not. And I think we should be respectful of the decisions made by each patient.

Identifying, recording, and transforming this pain is necessary for survival and for living without pain, and to help others who are victims of abusive relationships. This has been one of the main objectives of this book. The other has been to try to convey the importance of never surrendering to the fear, terror, suffering, and anger you feel when facing a disease as harsh as cancer.

A cancer diagnosis has usually been associated with death, and fear is heightened because, as Donna Orange's introductory phrase states: "Having the body invaded by something that grows and is mortally destructive evokes all early implicit memories of invasions, which are also devastating." Irvin Yalom, on the other hand, states that: "The anxiety of death can provoke an awakening to life." The fear of dying can be triggered after a loss (e.g., of a loved one, a job, a divorce, etc.), a disease, a trauma, or simply by the passage of time. Once we face our own mortality, we can reorganize our priorities, appreciate the beauty of life, and increase our willingness to take necessary risks for personal fulfillment. After this episode of her illness, Helen, and many other patients, have connected more with life or the meaning of life, living more in the present, the here and now. We know we are finite beings, and it's important that we learn to live in the fullest, happiest, most ethical, and meaningful way possible.

As we've been quoting throughout these pages, what heals is the relationship. Therefore, the empathetic, compassionate, understanding, human, vulnerable, and genuine attitude of the therapist forecasts "success" in the therapeutic space, creating a relational home supported by a "relational matrix" (Mitchell, 1987) conceptualized as a nurturing environment that facilitates the development of subjectivity from the beginning of life. Being human means being in relation to others. The relational matrix would be a mold or structure of connection to which human beings are rooted; it involves a dialectical tension between object relations and interpersonal relations, that is, between the intrapsychic and the interpersonal. The matrix is constituted by the participants, who, in turn, in a dialectical way, are shaped by this matrix. The matrix is the conceptual core of relational thinking, as it states that the psyche is constituted through the constant interaction between the Self, (oneself) the Other (object), and the space between them, or the interactive field.

I don't know if I've managed to reach one or both of the objectives of this small book; my humble intention was, and will remain for a long time, not to silence the pain nor give shelter to the devil, no matter how it dresses (even if it dresses in silk!). Therapists have a commitment to the suffering patient that goes far beyond individual or group therapies: it's the moment to NOT silence horror, barbarity, injustice, and cruelty. I think that as therapists and as human beings, we still have a lot to do. And above all, because we are aware that the law of silence is unhealthy, pathological, and generates suffering and symptoms. The law of truth, without pretense, stripped but clothed in emotion-suffering-pain-affects, is the way to freedom and mental health, to achieve an integrated Self (sense of Self). I quote a few phrases that Velasco mention in the final comment, which fit perfectly with the conclusion of the book: "In this case, writing, as well as verbalizing the damage Helen suffered in the present, is a form of acceptance of mental pain, a form of validation of the experience in the body, with a scar that condenses the memory of the damage suffered, but also the renewed possibility of authenticity, of truth."

This book also tries to be a song to freedom and equal conditions. I hope it has contributed a little, a grain of sand to achieve it. There is still a long way to go, but.... "We make the road by walking.... Blow by blow, verse by verse" (Machado, 1912).

No woman, no human being, should have to pay any price to be free and live in freedom. No one should lose a loved one due to a terrorist act, nor fear being a victim. A shout of condemnation to the helplessness felt before judicial injustice. Both Helen's case, and the Catalan politicians, and the sentence of "La Manada," primitive beings, instinctive like animals. And the courage one must have to bear our vulnerability and manage the intense fear and extreme fragility we feel when the devil dresses in cancer, or any disease that we have socially and historically associated with death in our collective unconscious.

We cannot allow any attack, any terrorist, unjust judge, or rapist, abuser to take away our dreams or our fight to pursue our dreams.

We will continue fighting, from our anonymity, with dignity, humility, compassion, respect, and coherence because freedom and human rights should be unquestionable and immovable standards, and free.

Invisibility can be felt as annihilation; no one can live without being seen by others. For this reason, from these lines, we want to give visibility to all that is invisible so that no one is left destroyed, devastated, and alone. We would like to see some of your thoughts to embrace them alongside ours, without being alone and annihilated. And give voice to all that is not heard because no one listens to it, not because it's not heard. Stop the pain of being deaf and try to prevent the devil from dressing in nothing but mutual respect, humility, generosity, kindness, understanding, justice, compassion, empathy, and genuineness.

And freedom exists and is forged free from the chains of anger.

What the hell!!

FROM THE PAIN TO GIVING MEANING: WORKING WITH TRAUMA THROUGH THE THERAPEUTIC RELATIONSHIP

Yanina Piccolo and Victoria Font Saravia

The deeply felt and profound ideas that we encounter when reading this book undoubtedly invite us to immerse ourselves in a universe of pain that cries out to find a place in the social fabric.

Pain seeps into each of us in different ways; it is inherent and inevitable for human beings, however, it will be tolerated in a unique way, depending on the circumstances in which each one finds themselves.

Pain and trauma should not be indissoluble. Every traumatic situation involves pain, but pain does not necessarily transform into trauma.

Trauma is the invisible pain in the world and in the Other, it is the silenced cry that still needs to be expressed and heard.

Returning to what was expressed on previous pages, it is essential to "give a voice to what is not heard, not because it cannot be heard, but because no one is listening."

In the exhibition "Poetry of Silence" (2023), Jaume Plensa poetically expresses this desperate silent cry of so many people who go through traumatic experiences without being able to hear, formulate, or express what they have experienced: 'and on which side of my body were you, my soul, that you did not help me'.

The author describes in detail in the book the traumatic experiences lived by Helen within her marriage. She also mentions the rape of a cousin in her childhood, an experience that was silenced by the entire family, transmuting her capacity for expression into taboo and silence, and preventing the possibility of metabolizing, formulating and, therefore, representing what happened. Her body, perhaps, sustained more than one traumatic story throughout her life.

Our body feels what happens to us before being able to give a personal meaning to the sensations (Donnel Stern, formulating the unformulated), even long before knowing it with words. The body also creates meanings; for this reason, it is not possible to work with trauma without working with body awareness, because trauma interrupts when the body feels. During the therapeutic process, we will collect the patient's own signals and those of the patient, building a choreography that will bring new meanings. In an attempt to remove the fear and suffering that is entrenched, in the words of the author, "A fear inscribed in the body."

Every painful situation that has not been validated in a containment space, that has not found a witness, a network that supports and holds, leaves the human being very alone and helpless, pushing him to over adapt as a necessary means of survival, thus generating a vicious circle where avoidance mechanisms are reinforced and ties with the environment are broken.

This is even more complex due to the current conditions in which we live. The current world is poor in voices and glances; the time of haste is not habitable and can leave us very alone. We see each other little, we love each other quickly, we stay little, we look hastily, we run more, we contemplate less, we hurt without time, many times there is no place for pain, to go deep, profound.

The psychological awakening that implies making a place for pain and trauma requires an emotional connection with others like us, with whom we manage to co-construct a relational context that holds and shelters as a home.

The pain of others awakens one's own, which is why denial is often activated as an anesthetic to pain. This is a mechanism that society and human beings tend to use. What is alarming is not measuring and underestimating the harmful power that denial generates.

At the other extreme, global crises, also sociocultural, open windows of hope. Feminist movements, for example, have rescued many frightened, ashamed, subjugated and abused women from pain and silence. This, undoubtedly, is a path that must continue to be paved day by day.

As mental health professionals, we have the opportunity to listen to and accompany others in their pain or in their traumatic experiences, knowing that we are entering into a task in itself, which is not at all simple.

This difficult and at the same time essential task forces us to be emotionally available, as well as trained in working with trauma.

An analyst who can tolerate suffering is involved in a different way. Their attitudes, and not just their words, will convey curiosity, excitement and hope. It will be a complex and integrative approach that will call upon the therapist to be very available in a sensitive and empathetic way, driven to integrate the experience at an emotional, mental and physical level.

Experiencing a new bond with these nuances paves the way in the process of feeling that it is worthwhile to build different ways of being in the world.

In this way, the psychotherapeutic relationship makes it possible for the traumatic experience that has been dissociated or remains unformulated to be articulated in such a way that it allows it to be thought about and mentalized, a witness to capture and feel what we have experienced. Being recognized by another enables the difficult work of bearing witness to our own pain.

It is essential that the therapist is in tune with his own body, since this provides him with a basis for not becoming deregulated while he tunes in with the patient's problems. It is not an easy task to tolerate the pain of trauma, being receptive to suffering. If the therapist does not achieve this connection with himself, it is possible that some selves that have become deregulated will fracture, dissociating from the intersubjective field. Therefore, we must not forget that being connected and involved in the patient's suffering opens the possibility of dissociation.

Therapy can act as a testimony and the therapist as a witness, encouraging self-observation and self-validation in the face of trauma, helping to identify what is harmful and discriminating nuances between attitudes that represent an attack on self-esteem and those that do not.

It is through witnessing that we come to know the experience as our own, this (the witnessing) develops in an interpersonal field, between two or more subjectivities.

When we listen to ourselves imaginatively or through the ears of the other (analyst) we perceive ourselves in a way that would not be possible in solitude.

We face the difficult question that people who have suffered trauma ask themselves: How do we construct the meaning of life? How do we recover motivation? How do we live without fear?

The search for meaning will be a long road that will undoubtedly have to be co-constructed, from a space that provides the support and security necessary to avoid confronting the patient with a new instance of retraumatization.

We are fortunate in our role of accompanying the pain of those who suffer and call upon us. We resonate, we grieve, we accommodate, and we try to sow hope in our dear patients from whom we learn so much.

EPILOGUE I
Concepció Garriga

I must begin by addressing the gender perspective. Dio Bleichmar (1997) stated that "girls and women are raised to accept violence in the name of love," and this violence—whether physical, psychological, or sexual—inflicts deep harm. Laura's work conveys the pain experienced by women and strives to overcome it.

In a previous work (Garriga, 2016), I noted that: "I view the gender perspective alongside the goal of gender equality as part of a broader cultural shift transforming industrial societies into democratic ones" (Welzel, 2014).

Velasco's biopsychosocial approach (2006, 2009) presents a perspective on the transition from traditional feminine subjectivity to an egalitarian model. With Helen's case and Laura's reflections supporting a more liberated, individuated, and self-realized subjective position, Laura advocates for an emancipatory egalitarian approach to development (Brandchaft, 2010).

Velasco (2006) argues that personal fulfillment (through work, knowledge, love, creation, etc.) is essential for health. Conversely, individuals in passive roles—serving others, socioeconomically disadvantaged, lacking recognition and appreciation, and struggling with relationship conflicts—experience a decline in ideals, sadness, loneliness, emptiness, rage, fear, and hatred, leading to symptoms such as anxiety and depression (Velasco, 2009). Helen clearly exhibits these characteristics. Laura's therapeutic work helps her transcend them, urging her with the mantra, "No surrender" (Springsteen, 1984). Laura motivates Helen to become a "subject" capable of creating her own future (Aron & Atlas, 2015) with her own "agency."

Laura's introductory poem, which expresses an assertive rather than aggressive vision of life, aligns with Benjamin's recent work (2018), emphasizing "equality, justice, freedom, security, strength, courage, hope, compassion, resilience, and coherence, free from anger, rancor, resentment, or pain." This vision promotes mutual recognition and a shift from the notion that "only one can survive" to a shared understanding of "we all deserve to live." Laura demonstrates her commitment to this approach by taking responsibility for herself, including what she gives and what she withholds (Garriga, 2014), resisting the hierarchical nature of patriarchal relationships (Gilligan & Richards, 2009).

EPILOGUE II
Alejandra Plaza Espinosa

Pain is Deaf and deafening is a volume in which Laura Molet guides us through crucial insights to understand pain. This book is essential reading for clinical psychoanalysis, illuminating how those in pain often find themselves in a tunnel that blocks their ability to hear others or even themselves. The intensity of pain can isolate individuals, causing a dissociative process that disrupts their connections.

A particularly striking aspect of the book is reflected in its title, which encapsulates the central idea that pain itself is deaf to the presence of others. Laura reveals that individuals in pain can be overwhelmed by "immense sadness, humiliation, rage, resentment, hatred, and a desire for revenge," which can distort their perception of what they are entitled to receive from those around them. This can lead to the victim becoming a victimizer. The fear of vulnerability inherent in this pain can drive individuals to become aggressive, erasing others and their subjectivity. Pain thus becomes all-consuming, silencing any internal dialogue and focusing solely on the suffering itself. Pain is deaf .. ., it doesn't let you listen to the other, feel connected. It not only erases the other, but it ends up erasing oneself. All the dimensions of who the subject is are nullified. The inner chorus falls silent because there is no one to listen, only pain remains.

This book prevents us from the dissociation that therapists might experience to avoid their own pain or that of their patients. This dissociation, while protective, can detach therapists from their patients' experiences. Laura's insights encourage staying engaged with others, as she does with Helen.

The narration of the book deafens us, we stop listening to others, we feel limited in connecting, in mutuality, in receiving and in giving.

Helen, with all her physical and emotional pain, embodies how terrible it is to be in a relationship where love turns into abuse. After accompanying Laura and Helen through this painful process, we begin to find hope in the relationship they establish.

Against dissociation, we have the strength of the relationship they create. Laura conveys to us the power of companionship, empathy, and being a witness to pain. This strength is rooted in knowing that the other is involved, feeling on the skin that the other has something at stake, and that what happens in the relationship matters. This intertwining of lives is a balm that helps to sustain life, as it happened with Helen in overcoming cancer.

As readers, we are witnesses to the experiences between Helen and Laura, and we feel involved with our own pain and with our bodies, with their own tears and their own repairs. With great sensitivity, Laura connected us with the suffering of the patient and with our own suffering as therapists. She genuinely and honestly shared her own experiences and pain. All of this became a tool for emotional work and reconstruction, both for the patient and for herself. The accompaniment was a fundamental process in transforming devastation into growth. In a very subtle way, Laura presents us with invaluable material for repair and help. Finally, the seed remains with us to learn how to restore life where there is suffering.

EPILOGUE III: NO SURRENDER

Summary of my participation in the IARPP International congress, held in June 2018. Part of it was published in La Vanguardia, after the attack perpetrated in Barcelona on August 17, 2017. Even though it was not recently written, I feel that it fits with the spirit of the book, and the message of strength, courage, of never giving up and of searching for freedom that emanates from the pages of this work that the reader has in his/her hands, and I think that makes it still relevant, unfortunately.

The political-social situation in Catalonia is very complex; we are living, or rather, suffering, a difficult divorce between Spain and Catalonia. This separation has directly to do with the divorce of my patient Helen—which I referred to in the second chapter—and the metaphor of her as Catalonia, and the husband as Spain—the oppressor. Peaceful politicians being unjustly imprisoned, political exiles, revolts, sociocultural and political instability repeating for the umpteenth time the same atrocities in my country, (Guerra dels segadors, 1714, 1936–39, post war...;[In Catalan we call "*Guerra dels segadors*" which means in English "The war of the reapers"]). For those interested in going deeper into this specific topic, I recommend you to read the paper my friend and colleague Concepció Garriga prepared for her conference at the IARPP-International congress on the political repression that is being experienced in Catalonia, entitled: "*The long journey of Catalonia to become an independent state. Its traumatic legacy and its resilient effects*" (Garriga, 2018).

Added to another judicial injustice, the case known as "*La manada*" (The Pack), in which an 18-year-old girl was raped by 5 men during the San Fermín festivities in July 2017; the resolution of Thursday, April 26, 2018, according to which some judges considered that there was no rape, but abuse! Protests in the streets, women and men together demanding justice in a deeply sexist and corrupt society. (This news deeply affected many people, in particular I talked about and developed the strong impact it had on my patient Helen).

Everything that is not a YES is a NO: only YES IS YES.

Any intrusion into a body naked of desire is rape.

From my own experience, and from other patients, I know well what it is to fight tirelessly for freedom. It is a long road. And the fight is so unnecessary and exhausting, when a divorce is not desired by both parties, as it is the case of Catalonia and Spain, or of any couple in disagreement... Then who sees themselves as the "powerful" wants to crush, destroy and annihilate that country or person, who only yearns for freedom. We have many historical and social examples, such as the struggle of Nelson Mandela, among the most famous known, or that of a group of anonymous students from East Germany who in the 1950s held a minute of silence, not authorized by the communist dictatorship, which was so wonderfully filmed in the movie *The Silent Revolution*. And sometimes, the actions, thoughts and initiatives that do not make noise end up being the loudest and most forceful.

It takes a lot of courage to live in fear. To accept our existential vulnerability, one has to be brave; the use of violence to achieve political, economic, or personal objectives is an attack, and is condemnable. And we raise our voices loud and clear to say, echoing Bruce Springsteen's spirit: we will not surrender.

We shouldn't have to pay any price to be free and live in freedom. We won't let our dreams be taken away from us.

We will fight with dignity and respect because human rights and freedom are, or should be, invincible.

FINAL COMMENT: INTEGRATED SENSE OF SELF

Rosa Velasco

Writing is a way of recording experiences, it is a way of accepting them and it is, without a doubt, a good way of validation.

This is a volume that brings all this together and according to my particular way of thinking about this book, this is an exercise that contributes to the construction of an integrated sense of self for the author as well for the readers and those who suffer to whom the message is addressed.

"I write to relieve those who suffer," says the author. She writes in order to repair the damage caused by the lack of validation of the suffered experience. This work would entail the differentiation of that past with this current present. What did not happen in the past, can finally happen now due to one's own initiative. At this moment, already with an already built professional identity and from that place, Laura Molet speaks to us about her patients and also about herself, implicitly and explicitly. In one of my papers, "*Working with the implicit*" (published in CeIR), I had the opportunity to comment that the line that separates the professional identity and the personal identity was very thin and that the clinical supervision that we carry out consisted precisely in this, being able to increase the levels of truth both to be able to have an authentic dialogue with oneself and to be able to dialogue in the intimate room of analysis with the analysand from the most genuine authenticity.

As psychoanalytic psychotherapists and due to the experience of personal analysis, clinical supervision and the work with patients, we know that a first step to move forward on the construction of an integrated sense of self is to be able to identify the experience in order to then validate the emotion that goes with it and to be able to metabolize it by transforming that emotion. Mental states are transitory, but if they persist over time or if a certain relational pattern predominates over the other possible ones, we will think that we could not or are not being able to "digest well" the sensation-feeling-thought, leading to high levels of dissatisfaction with the consequent anxiety of dys-regulated mood states. The body keeps score, as Van der Kolk refers to in his book, "The body keeps the score" on the emotional after-effects of trauma.

On this occasion, writing, as well as the verbalization of the damage suffered by Helen in the present, is a form of acceptance of mental pain, a form of validation of the experience in the body, with a scar that condenses the memory of the damage suffered but also the renewed possibility of authenticity, of truth. *Pain is deaf*, tells us about Helen's experience, which is an evolution of a first approximation. And as I have already expressed in "What is relational psychoanalysis? in search of a place in the world", we do not want indifference to win the battle because we need to "be seen" in another way, not as victims but as agents with initiatives that regulate our unique way of feeling.

To achieve having an integrated feeling of Self may take us a lifetime, in this path, we should increase the levels of truth: both in understanding of ourselves, as well as the understanding of our relationships with others, as the writer Carrere brilliantly expresses in his novel *Lives Other than My Own.*

In this brave initiative, Laura Molet writes about mental pain (the pain of oneself and others) helps us understand human emotional regulation and also shows us how a traumatic past can stop being unconsciously present in the present of our interactions. On this path we have changed, our feeling of self is now more integrated.

FINAL POEM

From the depths of time
you come, love, every morning
to sweetly tell me
the fragile sadness of the moment
the pale message of the ephemeral past
but I always have
the harpsichord
but I always have
the anemones
but I always have
the parentheses
but I always have
the firefly
in the depths of time
you walk, love, every morning
so that the moments and the ephemeral
stick the sting of the impossible
on the high tide
never lost of the hidden eternities
but you always have the heart.

Manuel de las Rivas, 2003 (unpublished)

REFERENCES

Aron, L.& Atlas, G. (2015). Generative enactment: Memories from the future, *Psychoanalytic Dialogues* 25(3):309- 324.

Aron & Atlas, G (2018). *Dramatic Dialogue: Contemporary Clinical Practice.* New York. Routledge.

Atlas, G. (2022). *Emotional Inheritance. A therapist, Her Patients and the Legacy of Trauma.* New York: Little, Brown Spark.

Ávila Espada, A. (2013). *La Tradición Interpersonal: Perspectiva Social y Cultural en Psicoanálisis.* Colección Pensamiento Relacional nº 8. Madrid: Ágora Relacional.

Barragán, M. (2020). ¿De quién era ese sentimiento de desesperanza? *Clínica e Investigación Relacional.* 14(1):103- 122.

Beebe, B., Jaffe, J., Markese, S., Buck, K., Chen, H., Cohen, P., Bahrick, L., Andrews, H., & Feldstein, S. (2010). The origins of 12-month attachment: A microanalysis of 4-month mother-infant interaction. *Attachment & Human Development, 12*(1-2):6–141. https://doi.org/10.1080/14616730903338985

Benjamin, J. (2018). *Beyond Doer and Done To. Recognition, Theory, Intersubjectivity and The Third.* New York: Routledge.

Boston Change Process Study Group (2008). Change in Psychotherapy. A Unifying Paradigm. New York: W.W. Norton.

Brandchaft, B. Doctors, S., & Porter, D. (2010). *Toward an Emancipatory Psychoanalysis.* New York: Routledge.

Bromberg, P. (2011). *The Shadow of The Tsunami and The Growth of Relational Mind*. New York: Routledge.

Carr, R. (2011). Combat and human existence. Toward an intersubjective approach to combat-Related PTSD. *Psychoanalytic Psychology* 28 (4)471-496.

Coderch, J. Plaza, Alejandra (2016). *Emoción y relaciones humanas: El psicoanálisis relacional como Terapéutica social*. Madrid: Ágora Relacional.

——— (2012). *Realidad, Interacción y Cambio Psíquico: La Práctica de la Psicoterapia Relacional II*. Colección pensamiento relacional n°15. Madrid: Ágora Relacional.

——— (2017). Las experiencias terapéuticas modifican el inconsciente relacional. *VII Jornadas IARPP-E. Barcelona*, 1 de abril de 2017.

——— (2018). *Las Experiencias Terapéuticas en el Proceso Psicoanalítico.: Un Estudio Del Cambio Psíquico Desde la Teoría De los Sistemas Intersubjetivos, No Lineales y Dinámicos*. Madrid: Ágora Relacional.

Buechler, S. (2015). *Marcando la Diferencia en la Vida de los Pacientes. Experiencia Emocional en el* Ámbito *Terapéutico*. Madrid: Ágora Relacional.

Dio Bleichmar, E. (1997). *La Sexualidad Femenina: De la Niña a la Mujer*. Barcelona: Paidós.

Doctors, S. (2013). Perspectivas de apego en el trabajo clínico con adolescentes y sus figuras parentales: el uso del cuerpo para regular la emoción. *IV Jornadas IARPP en Barcelona*. Mayo 2013.

Fonagy, P. (2001). *Teoría del apego y psicoanálisis*. Barcelona: Espaxs, 2004.

Font Saravia, V. Forli, M. Mayorga, P. & Piccolo, Y. (2021). *Psicoanálisis Relacional: Una nueva mirada, una nueva práctica.* Buenos Aires: Letra Viva.

Garriga, C. (2014). La bondad y la ética del cuidado en la subjetividad femenina. Implicaciones del DSM-V para la sexualidad de las mujeres. *Aperturas Psicoanalíticas* 46.

----(2016). Aportaciones desde la perspectiva de género al caso clínico... *Clínica e Investigación Relacional* 10(2):477-489.

Garriga, C. (2018). El largo viaje de Catalunya para convertirse en un estado independiente: su herencia traumática y sus efectos resilientes. Congreso IARPP, junio, Nueva York.

Gilligan, C. & Richards. D.A.J. (2009). The Deepening Darkness: Patriarchy, Resistance and Democracy's Future. New York: Cambridge University Press.

Guerra Cid, L.R. (2018). *Palos en las Ruedas*: Una Perspectiva Relacional y Social Sobre por qué el Trauma nos Impide Avanzar. Barcelona: Editorial Octaedro, S.L.

Golder, V. (2004). When love hurts: Treating abuse relationships. *Psychoanalytic Inquiry* 24:346-372.'

Kahlo, F. http://es.wikipedia.org/wiki/ Frida Kahlo

——— http://www.revistasculturales.com/a/372/1/frida-Kahlo-la-frente-y-el-perfil.htm

Kandinsky, W (1979). *De lo Espiritual en el Arte: La Nave de los Locos.* Mexico, D.F.: Premia Editora.

Larsson, S (2005). *Los Hombres que no Amaban a las Mujeres,* transl. M. Lexell y J.J. Ortega Román. Colección Áncora y Delfín, Vol. 112. Barcelona: Ediciones Destino.

Leuzinger-Bohlebler, M. (2012). Changes in dreams–From a psychoanalysis with a traumatized, chronic depressed patient. In P. Fonagy, H. Kächele, M. Leuzinger-Bohlebler, Eds., *The*

Significance of Dreams. Bridging Clinical and Extraclinical Research in Psychoanalysis, pp. 49–85. London: Karnac.

Lijtmaer, R. (2017). Mass migration: Hope or dread? Conferencia IARPP Internacional Nueva York, junio 2018.

Márai, S. (1999). *La* Última *Trovada*. Barcelona: Ediciones Salamandra.

Marrone, M. (2001). *La Teoría del Apego: Un Enfoque Actual.* Madrid: Prismática.

Molet, L. (2012). Atreverse a ser: Reunión anual. IARPP-E. 13 y 14 de abril de 2012, Sevilla. *Clínica e Investigación Relacional* Vol. 7(1).

——— (2013). Rompiendo el sistema de acomodación patológica. IV Congreso IARPP-E, 25 de mayo, Barcelona. *Clínica e Investigación Relacional* Vol. 7(3), octubre 2013, pp. 594-601.

——— (2013). Trauma relacional: Rompiendo el sistema de acomodación patológica. Congreso IARPP-International. Chile, noviembre de 2013.

Montero, R. (2013). *La Ridícula Idea de no Volver a Verte.* Barcelona: Ediorial Seix Barral.

Morrison, A. (1997). *La Cultura de la Vergüenza*: *Anatomía de un Sentimiento Ambiguo.* Barcelona: Paidós Contextos.

Orange, D. (2011). Orange, D.M. (2011). "La actitud de los héroes": Bernard Brandchaft y la hermenéutica de la confianza. *Clínica e Investigación Relacional* 5 (3): 507-515. .

——— (2013). *El Desconocido que Sufre.* Santiago de Chile: Editorial do los Cuatro Vientos.

——— Atwood, G.E. y Stolorow, R.D. (1997). *Trabajando Intersubjetivamente. Contextualismo en la Práctica Psicoanalítica.* Madrid: Ágora Relacional.

Riera, R. (2010). *La Conexión Emocional*. Barcelona: Editorial Octaedro.

Stern, D.B. (1997). *Unformulated Experience: From Dissociation to Imagination in Psychoanalysis*. Hillsdale, NJ: Analytic Press.

——— (2021). *La Infinidad de lo no Dicho*. Lima: Editorial Gradiva.

Stolorow, R. (2013). Teoría de los sistemas intersubjetivos. Una perspectiva psicoanalítica fenomenológica contextualista. Psychoanalytic Dialogues. Vol. 23 nº 4.

——— (2012). "De la mente al mundo, de la pulsión al afecto: Una perspectiva fenomenológico-contextual en Psicoanálisis". *Clínica e Investigación Relacional 5* Vol 6(3). Octubre 2012, pp 381-395.

——— (2015). Pain is not pathology. Presentation London 14-17 May 2015. World Congress for Existential Therapy.

——— & Atwood, G.E. (1992). *Los Contextos del Ser: Las Bases Intersubjetivas de la Vida Psíquica*. Barcelona: Herder, 2004.

Vargas, R. (2022). *La Piel Del Mundo: Una Mirada del Psicoanálisis Relacional A Las Familias Contemporáneas*. Seville: Caligrama Editorial.

Velasco, R. (2002). El sentimiento de sí y el afecto de vergüenza. *Intersubjetivo*. 4(2):287-294.

——— (2014). Arte para dar cuenta del dolor del pasado: Comentario a: Lágrimas de dolor y de belleza de M. Eigen. *Clínica e Investigación Relacional* 8(2):351-358.

Velasco, S. (2006). Atención Biopsicosocial al Malestar de las Mujeres. Madrid, Instituto de la Mujer, Salud, 9.

——— (2009). *Sexos, Género y Salud: Teoría y Métodos para la Práctica Clínica y Programas de Salud*. Madrid: Minerva Ediciones.

Villanueva, C. (2023). Consideraciones sobre el perdón. Presentado en el congreso de Psicoanálisis de la UIC Universidad Intercontinental de México, en 2023.

Wallin, D. (2012). *El Apego en Psicoterapia*. Bilbao: Desclée de Brower.

——— (2014). Heridas que deben servir de herramientas: la historia de apego del terapeuta como fuente de impasse y de inspiración.

Welzel, C. (2014*). Freedom Rising: Human Empowerment and the Quest for Emancipation.*: Cambridge: Cambridge University Press.

Yalom, I. (2021). *Mirar al Sol.* Barcelona: Ediciones Destino.